YEATS AT HIS LAST

STANLEY SULTAN

NEW YEATS PAPERS

GENERAL EDITOR: LIAM MILLER

The Dolmen Press New Yeats Papers form a continuing series in which each paper deals with some aspect of Yeats's life, work and background. Each paper is published as a separate volume, complete in itself and presents an authoritative study of its subject. The format of the series is quarto, with a page size of 10 by 7 inches, and illustrations and facsimiles are included where relevant. Each Paper is sewn and covered in limp boards.

Titles already Published

Subject to an additional 6.75% V.A.T. surcharge in the Republic of Ireland.

NEW YEATS PAPERS XI

STANLEY SULTAN

YEATS AT HIS LAST

THE DOLMEN PRESS

CONTENTS

General Editor : Liam Miller

ILLUSTRATIONS

Grateful acknowledgement is made to Miss Anne Yeats and to The Cuala Press Limited for permission to reproduce :

ⓒ Stanley Sultan 1975
ISBN 0 85105 271 1

Printed and published in the Republic of Ireland at the Dolmen Press, North Richmond Industrial Estate, North Richmond Street, Dublin 1. First published 1975.
Distributed in the United States of America and in Canada by Humanities Press Inc., 171 First Avenue, Atlantic Highlands, N.J. 07716.

Drawing by Jack B. Yeats, R.H.A.,
from the front cover of *On the Boiler*, The Cuala Press, 1939.

I

During its early stages the familiar final lyric in Yeats's *Last Poems and Plays* and *Collected Poems* was called 'Creed,' and consisted of a series of assertions each beginning with the words 'I believe.' Plainly, his evolution of that into 'Yeats's testament' to other Irish artists was an improvement; yet their self-appointed master's five-part bequest in as many of the six numbered sections of 'Under Ben Bulben,' that quintet of clusters of doctrinal assertion which is the body of the poem, is not very different in general design from his original 'Creed.' The major change, reinforced when he discarded a second for its eventual title, was his giving the body a head.

With the brief introductory section repeating its imperative 'Swear,' Yeats's testament poem became a dramatic monologue. And as a result, although the finished 'Under Ben Bulben' does incorporate his testament — both will and witness — it beggars that familiar characterization of it. The poem is a direct injunction, arrogant because he is not the murdered king of Denmark seeking revenge, but having the ancient power of law because in historical fact he does speak, as the end of 'Under Ben Bulben' declares and that eventual title emphasizes, from the grave. Their *seanchan* commands Irish 'poet and sculptor' to 'swear' by the gnosis 'the sages spoke' and 'swear' by the 'company' of immortal Irish, both hypostatized in the legacy of doctrine he has left them. His adding the introductory section was a dramatic *coup*; and if it makes 'Under Ben Bulben' somewhat too histrionic for a valedictory, that is because the poem is, despite the standard editions, a prologue.

Not surprisingly, he devotes the central section of the testamentary five to art. And he tells his heirs 'Measurement began our might,' then traces the history of the plastic arts in Western civilization from the statues of Phidias, through the Sistine Chapel ceiling of 'Michael Angelo,' through post-Renaissance deterioration only partly relieved by Blake and certain other visionary artists, to a present nadir : what began in 'measurement' has ended in 'confusion' ('Confusion fell upon our thought').

7

The value of the passage as cultural history, or as philosophy of art, or even for appraisal of the virtues and faults of Yeats's own poems, plays, or stories, is questionable. But reiterations he made elsewhere, and especially its context, indicate that he is deeply sincere. He scarcely would be facetious, impetuous or even undecided in demanding the allegiance of others to a formulation of 'His Convictions' (the second title) made when he was near death. And the passage tells us that he considers activities of the artist he describes as 'measurement,' and as 'thought' that abhors 'confusion,' to be indispensable for — if not the source of — 'might.'

Reflective readers of the works of Yeats have been aware of his Romantic dimension, critics are increasingly concerned with it, and Harold Bloom's recent book *Yeats* (Oxford, 1970) makes an eloquent case that he was 'the last of the High Romantics.' Nevertheless, as early as 1900, in the first paragraph of 'The Symbolism of Poetry,' he derided the belief that 'people have no imagination who do not write without forethought and afterthought'; and two years later, in 'Adam's Curse,' he described the labour of making poems as harder than scrubbing a kitchen pavement or breaking stones ('A line will take us hours maybe').

Good artists of whatever persuasion work hard and use their minds, of course. But Romantic artists do not characteristically stress that fact. Unless Yeats was ignorant of his true and sole affinity his express 'conviction' in 'Under Ben Bulben,' held through most of his career, affirms other dimensions of his art. So does his practice; those jottings of prose statement he worked up and up into great poems come immediately to mind. One cannot merely dismiss the fact that in IV of 'Under Ben Bulben' he chose to use the words 'thought' and 'measurement' and to create a certain emphasis.

'Long-Legged Fly' and 'The Statues' are a pair of poems both of which seem anticipated in that passage, although the composition of the three poems during his last year of life overlapped, and the pair were completed before 'Under Ben Bulben.' * In 'Long-Legged

---

*Jon Stallworthy, *Vision and Revision in Yeats's Last Poems* (Oxford : Clarendon Press, 1969), pp. 115, 122-23, 151; and Curtis Bradford, *Yeats's 'Last Poems' Again*, Dolmen Press Centenary Papers VIII (1965), 259-88, 285-86. This

Fly' he speaks of the movements of Michelangelo's hand under the ceiling of the Sistine Chapel not in terms of Imagination or Genius but as the manifestation of 'his mind'; and in its companion poem 'measurement' has become 'numbers' and 'calculations,' while the contrary 'confusion' has become the 'formless' fruit of 'Asiatic vague immensities.'

Appropriately, as 'The Statues' moves into one of those Yeatsian conclusions of virtuoso drumbeat oratory it presents again, in catalogue, all the terms signifying artistic 'might':

> When Pearse summoned Cuchulain to his side,
> What stalked through the Post Office? What intellect,
> What calculation, number, measurement, replied?

For in that difficult lyric the old poet expounded his testament about art.

'The Statues' serves the present concern well in two ways: it identifies clearly the contrary traditions Yeats posits; and it defines the role of that 'intellect,' 'number,' he insists is instrumental in 'our' proper one. In 'The Single Image,' the final chapter of his study of the development of Yeats's aesthetic, *The Vast Design* (Univ. of Toronto Press, 1964), Edward Engelberg presents 'The Statues' as the culminating statement of the social thinker as well as the artist, a poem which 'celebrates' the integration of 'the single, conscious, countable and measurable image of art' with 'the vast design of history . . . which it conquers' (p. 204). The perception that it celebrates an integration of opposites which is crucial for both art and

---

study is indebted to those two works, especially the second, at a number of points; but aside from the identifying of quotations, my practice will be to cite works on Yeats only to provide supporting evidence for assertions of possibly unfamiliar fact, as in the present case. The process of assimilating ourselves to Yeats's poetry is an accretive one, and few people can have written anything of value about it not informed by reading in scholarship and criticism which began with one's first baffled youthful fascination. Although much of whatever erudition this study seems to have was culled, and although critical works as well were of indispensable benefit, documentation of all my indebtedness would be distracting more than anything else, if it were possible, and I offer the present declaration in its place.

society is a valuable one. However, the role it assigns to 'number,' the 'countable and measurable' element in 'our' art, is successful integration not with human 'history' but with the element within art itself that is opposite to 'intellect' or 'number.'

The contrary traditions are more easily dealt with. Not surprisingly, the poem declares that our Western one is that of the now 'unfashionable gyre' ('The Gyres'); it has undergone the virtual eclipse recapitulated in 'Under Ben Bulben' beneath the inexorable ascendancy of the objective 'Asiatic' tradition which once had been 'put off' with the statues of Phidias. It is embodied in the legacy of Cuchulain, the patriotism and appreciation for the Irish heritage of Pearse who 'summoned' him, the violence of the Easter Rising (all of which also are articles of the poet's testament in 'Under Ben Bulben'). And 'we' continue faithful to it, the remainder of that last stanza asserts :

> We Irish, born into that ancient sect
> But thrown upon this filthy modern tide
> And by its formless spawning fury wrecked,
> Climb to our proper dark, that we may trace
> The lineaments of a plummet-measured face.

Stoically so. For the faithfulness of the (true) Irish not only produced a late flowering of the art of their way — the statue of Cuchulain that commemorates the Rising (and which will not bear the weight Yeats has imposed on it) — but also dooms them in the 'formless . . . fury' of the present age. They are the last vestige of the 'Europe' which Yeats opposes to 'formless' 'Asia,' whose art (along with its politics, religion, epistemology, etc.) has otherwise conquered the West — for the time being.

It may be recalled that in *On the Boiler*, the polemical pamphlet which he wrote during this time, Yeats reiterates his thesis about the two antithetical traditions :

> There are moments when I am certain that art must once again accept those Greek proportions which carry into plastic art the Pythagorean numbers, those faces which are divine because all there is empty and measured. Europe was not born when Greek

galleys defeated the Persian hordes at Salamis[;] but when the Doric studios sent out those broadbacked marble statues against the multiform, vague, expressive Asiatic sea, they gave to the sexual instinct of Europe its goal, its fixed type.[1]

The phrase 'the sexual instinct of Europe' has a wider reference than to Europe's artists alone. And Yeats's meaning is clarified by a teaching of the protagonist of his early play, *The King's Threshold*. The tag-named Seanchan teaches his pupils that poetry is vital to society because :

> the poets hung
> Images of the life that was in Eden
> About the child-bed of the world, that it,
> Looking upon those images, might bear
> Triumphant children.[2]

The kinship with the beginning of IV of 'Under Ben Bulben,' in which 'Poet and sculptor' are commanded to 'Make [man] fill the cradles right,' is apparent. The testament about art and both the poems that elucidate it all actually represent art as even more crucial to human generation; but that must be considered in its proper context. Here, the relevant reference of the phrase 'the sexual instinct of Europe' is to Europe's artists.

The passage in *On the Boiler* is worth quoting less because it distinguishes again Yeats's right tradition in art and his wrong one, than because with the presence of that phrase it makes explicit his complementary point about art in 'The Statues': the role he assigns to 'intellect,' 'Pythagorean numbers.' As the first stanza of 'The Statues' tells us more obliquely, 'numbers' itself is not the great achievement. That achievement, 'our' proper art, is the sculptor's proceeding from 'numbers' into a creation which integrates 'numbers' with its very opposite, his native 'sexual instinct,' presumably in synergy, the Yeatsian antinomial consort. Thus, the poem says that the people did not stare at the statues in that ancient agora because of Pythagoras's concepts; they stared because the sexual imaginations of the sculptors used those concepts to create austere classical works which also were endowed with 'character.' And in order to emphasize that he means not broadly 'sensual' but explicitly sexual imagination, he makes the shocking point that boys and girls, since they created sexual fantasies while masturbating, had no need to 'stare'; for they recognized the source of the 'character' which the sculptors brought to bear on Pythagoras's 'numbers' in the statues. With the experience of their beds, the boys and girls responded to the statues as products of sexual imagination embodying the reciprocal power of the art it creates:

> But boys and girls, pale from the imagined love
> Of solitary beds, knew what they were,
> That passion could bring character enough,
> And pressed at midnight in some public place
> Live lips upon a plummet-measured face.

Alert for the influence of Yeats's romantic antecedents, some have seen a significant similarity between the first dozen words above and the 'moment of desire' passage in Blake's *Visions of the Daughters of Albion*. But including the psychological etiology Blake provides (repression), that passage has a closer kinship with a more recent work, a popular novel by Philip Roth. My apparently facetious observation is intended to discredit a comparison which would both confuse the argument and alter the effect of Yeats's poem. For it would blunt the thrust of his boldly cool illustration of the power of the sexual imagination. That incontrovertible illustration out of human experience is what he gives us, and not a pointless echo of Blake's sermon against imposed continence. (Even the elements in common—adolescents fantasizing and masturbating in bed—though he must have read them in Blake once, also can be said to be in the public domain.)

In recent years critics have been stressing more than ever the importance Yeats gave to sexuality in his mature thought. The sexual imagination has a special relevance to figure sculpture, of course. But he both selected and used repeatedly 'those broad-backed marble statues' as his illustration of the genesis of 'Europe's' proper art in general. So something very close to the sexual imagination would be the source of the 'character' which the poet as well must combine with 'calculation' in his work.

If my understanding of it is adequate to what the old Yeats wrote about art in 'The Statues' and elsewhere, and if his actual created work reflects his 'conviction' to the extent suggested by the role 'calculation' played in the final state of 'Under Ben Bulben,' then to call his work essentially romantic is to comprehend it — in either sense of the word — no more than to call it essentially the opposite. For the artistic doctrine which Ireland's master poet apparently evolved and saw fit to bequeath to his heirs has at its centre both 'intellect' or 'calculation' and 'the sexual instinct' of (he no doubt would say) their 'race.'

That word already was long a political one when Yeats was writing the works that have been mentioned, and all but 'Long-Legged Fly' have their provocative political components. In the pair of lines in 'The Statues' quoted above about 'this filthy modern tide' and 'its formless spawning fury,' for example, the poet's iambic and tropologic control of his invective almost legitimized the meaning, but perhaps not quite.

To avoid its hovering presence over the rest of this essay, the aging Yeats's sometimes truly obnoxious (much of it is merely Old Tory) politics had best be brought openly into context here. A documented exposition and critique of Yeats's politics would be a major digression. Besides, it could add little to Conor Cruise O'Brien's fine essay 'Passion and Cunning : Politics of Yeats,' in the volume edited by A. N. Jeffares and K. G. W. Cross, *In Excited Reverie* (New York : Macmillan, 1965). Rather, what seems relevant and necessary at this point is the making of a statement of record, to obviate any question about my own politics which might otherwise compromise my discussion of the old Yeats's work and thought. The problem is a real one. For writers on Yeats have ranged from one extreme of politically-orientated moralists who are blind to his achievement, to the other extreme of snobs and cold-warriors who attribute prophetic political wisdom to him.

Even reasonable positions differ. Quite rightly, Professor Bloom opposes himself to 'those Yeats critics who admire everything in Yeats' (p. 435). And yet his corrective appraisals of 'Under Ben

Bulben' and 'The Statues' exceed the mark because political indignation has drawn the bowstring too far; for example, although 'The Statues' is far from the 'superb' poem some have called it, its first and last stanzas are too rich for it to be simply, as he says, 'bad.' I am less indignant than Professor Bloom, but more so than Northrop Frye, who in the memorable essay reprinted in his *Fables of Identity* (New York: Harcourt, Brace and World, 1963), 'Yeats and the Language of Symbolism,' dismisses the poet's 'social and political dithering' (p. 236). My opinion of Yeats's politics most approximates to those put into print by his fellow-Irishmen O'Casey, MacNeice and Dr. O'Brien.

In my opinion, 'Under Ben Bulben' and 'The Statues' together comprise and *On the Boiler* expounds a set of repellent political attitudes which, if they cannot with full justice be associated with those of Alfred Rosenberg, cannot be fully exonerated either. Yeats seems to me no more racist than Arthur Koestler when he asserts a preference for Western habits of thinking and ways of perceiving to Eastern ones. But: he sees these as racial traits with the other threatening his own; he sets the Irish apart as a superior 'folk'; he opposes modern democratic society; he glorifies a heroic primitive national past; above all, he sincerely advocates both eugenics and violence. I regard the incongruities with fascist thought as no less fundamental, however: his attitudes toward art, a hereditary aristocracy, industrialism, centralized urban government. Even the reason he gives for advocating violence — in a *sententia* fondly reclaimed word for word from Michael Robartes in the second section of *A Vision* — dangerously foolish though it was in 1938, is melioristic: 'Love war *because of* its horror, *that belief may be changed*, civilisation renewed' (p. 20, emphasis mine).

Reading in *On the Boiler* of 'inferior stocks' and 'uneducable masses,' one recalls with delight the discussion of 'good breeding' by another of the 'indomitable Irishry' — Shaw's humane, witty and democratic rejection of totalitarian eugenics almost four decades before, in John Tanner's 'Revolutionist's Handbook.' (In the same piece he wrote of 'such monsters as the tramp and the gentleman'; that Yeats dreamed he was a sewing machine is a libel but no surprise). And yet alongside that obnoxious stuff Yeats offers perceptions about the influence of cultural or physical environment that reveal powerful insight and contradict his argument.

Although this study must be concerned with the old Yeats's doctrines, it is not about them. Furthermore, only his conception of the essence of proper art is important at the moment, and that only because of one of its two antithetical emphases: 'measurement,' 'calculation,' 'intellect.' My intention has been to establish beyond dispute that the last of the High Romantics himself directs one to look for very different qualities in his work. My reason is because those qualities seem to inform his final work so superbly. This study is about a neglected artistic achievement of that anachronistic, snobbish, reactionary, bigoted intellect, its shaping the volume which — fittingly — was composed in the year of *On the Boiler* and includes all three poems. The standard editions that totally transpose 'Under Ben Bulben' from initial to final position in that volume present a mere grotesque. The authentic *Last Poems* seems to me a moving triumph of the dying poet, a figurative urn for his ashes most becoming to them and literally well wrought.

II

The recent demonstrations of Yeats's romantic dimension have been just and necessary; the very different and long familiar qualities to which he himself drew attention are additional to those of the Romantic. In other words, I am not proposing a simple alternative view of his poetry. What I am proposing is that to value the achievements of the Yeats of measurement-calculation-intellect more highly than has been the recent practice, is to appreciate more — in the full primary sense of the word — certain of his poetry, including *Last Poems*.

It must be said first that neglect of those achievements antedates preoccupation with the Romantic. The most relevant proof is that not until some time after Yeats's death did a critic first remark that 'he didn't accumulate poems, he wrote books'[3]; yet the process of calculation by which their creator had selected poems or set them aside for later use, and had ordered them in individual volumes which he often began with special introductory poems and even anticipated in the final poems of preceding (in some cases they were also complementary) volumes, goes back as far as *The Rose* in his *Poems* of 1895.

Sometimes this kind of calculation accomplishes little besides the satisfying coherence found in the simple sonnet 'sequence' (or in a similar contemporaneous volume such as Lawrence's *Look! We Have Come Through!*). But sometimes the case is more like when Sidney interrupts the sonnets of *Astrophel and Stella* at points of heightened intensity with songs, or Donne in *La Corona* weaves for religious offering a crown of sonnets celebrating the major events in the reign of Christ his king. Then the calculations of Yeats's intellect achieve a different order of richness in his art.

No longer unaware that 'he wrote books,' a reader of our day might recognize such achievement, yet disdain it as having little value. Textual evidence for the true *Last Poems* was published more than a decade ago.[4] But the volume which W. B. Yeats actually composed has been ignored or disregarded in the major studies of his poetry done since.[5] In this case, neglect of what may have been achieved by calculation would seem to be the direct result of current critical interest in the romantic Yeats and literal devaluation of his very different qualities.

Whether an achievement of calculation is properly valued by any particular reader or not (even whether or not he really notices most aspects of it) probably depends on his hierarchy of values *as* reader, especially on what he believes to be the most valuable quality and function of poetry. And to argue for a more inclusive view of Yeats's art in *Last Poems* I shall have to deal with this broader issue.

Some readers of poetry would dismiss my earlier suggestion that those two calumnious lines in 'The Statues' possibly are redeemed by their extended metaphor and the rhythm of their invective, as being a puerile argument that their 'form' may have altered their manifest and explicit meaning. That is not true, but is not claimed: the redemption came, if at all, through a change Yeats effected in the *status* of the meaning — through a subversion of its lexical potency.

Writing of 'creative conflict' or 'the tension of opposites' in romantic theory, W. K. Wimsatt quotes from a newspaper account of a middle-aged man who, aroused by a young girl's knitting, followed and murdered her. He then quotes two apt 'proverbs' in Blake's *Marriage of Heaven and Hell*:

He who desires but acts not, breeds pestilence.
Sooner murder an infant in its cradle than nurse unacted desires.

and cites as the canny 'verbal achievement' of the second that 'the starkness of a choice is covered in the word *nurse*.'[6]

By criticizing an almost imperative moral restraint with that word, Blake made its alternative more palatable; and the effect combines with other conditions his poem creates for the proverb to render benign, *within the poem*, the proposition acted on by the middle-aged man, whose moral implications on its very face are outrageous. The 'creative conflict' was achieved by subversion of the lexical potency of all but one word of the proverb. A similar diminution in the status of their meaning happens to many of the passages expressing obnoxious politics in *Last Poems*, possibly including the two lines in 'The Statues.'

However, meaning in a poem can have a mutable status (and the preposition can be 'in' not 'of') only if it has subordinate value, as it does to me. In other words, whether a reader appreciates such a subversion of the potency of meaning in one of Yeats's poems or regards it instead as Yeats's inconsistent treatment, either irrelevance or artistic weakness, depends on how important he considers meaning in poetry to be. And like how important a reader considers the achievements of calculation to be, that attitude is precisely an expression of values. Furthermore, the same individual who would regard my attitude toward meaning in poetry as pernicious or frivolous would tend to disdain what I call the achievements of calculation in poetry as frivolous or trivial. It is the fact that the two judgements are likely to go together that is most significant for the recent critical neglect of the authentic *Last Poems*. Both judgements express the same set of values; and the difference between his sort of readers and mine is fundamental.

The one sort read and value poetry chiefly for (conceive as its most valuable quality and function) *what it discloses beyond itself;*

the other sort read and value it chiefly for *what it works within itself*. The relative words 'chiefly' and 'most' are important, and no one need vulgarize the distinction between these attitudes by hating Donne in the former case or Shelley in the other. But it is real. The probable greater interest of a practising critic among the former sort of readers in a poet's whole corpus or a poetic tradition, that of one among my sort in individual artifacts, and generally the kind of job each sets himself to doing, proceeds naturally from the two contrasting fundamental attitudes toward poetry. That the former individuals treat meaning as embodied in a poem while the latter treat it as employed by the poem is a direct function of the same contrasting attitudes. So too are the differing responses to graces of calculation, such things as wit and formal arrangement usually affecting less what a poem discloses than what it works. Possibly, the now ascendant and the old once New systems of critical formulation which can be associated with the two attitudes respectively are less the foundations than the intellectual extrapolations of those attitudes, and temperament is as crucial to one's poetics as it is to one's politics.

Some have made pejorative historical associations, but the former sort of criticism is immeasurably more sophisticated and enlightening than the practice of those influence hunters and humanist critics of decades ago; its contributions, theoretical and practical, have advanced all our understanding of the relationships within literature both as a development through time and as an existent verbal realm, and so have put us all in its debt. Still, possessing fine ears, and willing to remark melody and rhythm, its representatives seem really to listen to individual works only for how the words go and what the song is about. Their interest is in the poet's perception of this world and his vision beyond it, any kinship to other poets' perceptions and visions respectively, and the two orders of reality themselves. Readers of that sort see part or all of a poet's corpus as admirable when it is — figuratively, at least — mystical, embodying and so leading to a truth beyond finite and/or mundane experience. And readers of my sort admire a poet's accomplishment in each work which is magical, achieving a power within itself.

The poets accommodate us both, of course; and Yeats, who is as

18

much Hic as Ille, Swan as Shadow, artisan as visionary, supremely so. We must not fail to accommodate all of him. Although awareness of his place in the tradition of apocalyptic Romanticism may cause one to ignore, for example, the pointed commentary he makes on it at the very start of his career (in the second of the pair of poems that begin *Collected Poems*, 'The Sad Shepherd'), he does have his place in it. Only, the obsessive images and other elements of Yeats the visionary are also artistic working, a wizard's conjuration, magic in a web of words. His art proceeds from the intellect of the magus as well as from the vision of the mystic; and only that more inclusive view of it can truly appreciate it.

As the literature of Modernism moves into perspective, it is revealing itself to be not so much the faithful expression of the new antithetical attitudes to Romanticism out of which it was created, as the dialectical offspring of both Romanticism and those attitudes. (Consider, for example, the role of the artist's inner life in the work of Proust, Strindberg, Joyce, Pirandello, Pound, Kafka, Eliot.) In the shaping of his last volume Yeats accomplished a triumph, a conjuration of vital power, which confirms him as the first of the High Modernists. In whatever measure this really is antithetical to his other identity, so much would his accomplishment please him.

III

Once neglected because of ignorance, that shapeliness, the dying magus's bequest to all of us, now seems to be the victim of indifference; to this point I have been trying to present some of the grounds for greater attention to it. Its initial concealment was the work of the familiar standard editions, *Last Poems and Plays* (1940) and *Collected Poems* (1950 and later), which place 'Under Ben Bulben' at the end of Yeats's 'lyrical' poems. They also: (1) combine as '*Last Poems*' the volume *New Poems* (1938) and the poems in *Last Poems and Two Plays* (1939) of the Cuala Press; (2) print the latter group of poems in an unnamed editor's sequence; and (3) insert near the end three additional poems from *On the Boiler*.

19

That what is designated '*Last Poems*' in these editions really does at least bibliographical violence to the canon of Yeats's poetry is suggested by the fact that he supervised the publications of his sister Elizabeth's Cuala Press, and by the case of the three poems taken from their contexts in *On the Boiler*. Presumably those three poems were not excluded from the Cuala Press *Last Poems and Two Plays* because of their appearance in Yeats's 'occasional' (he did not live to do a second) pamphlet. For *Purgatory*, which first appeared there, was included. Thus, the personae of the poems, two mad (in both senses) old men and Crazy Jane, are fully appropriate to *On the Boiler* and not at all to *Last Poems*; and in other respects the poems belong where the Cuala Press put them.[7]

The external evidence confirming the authenticity of the Cuala Press volume and its ordering of the poems as against the standard editions includes: (1) the independent publication of *New Poems* during Yeats's lifetime; (2) the advertisement of both *New Poems* and *Last Poems* (*sic*) in the Cuala Press list in *On the Boiler*, the abortive first edition of which seems to have been either completed or very nearly so during his life,[8] so that that short-form title is no editor's catch-all but, with the living poet's authority, designates a distinct volume of poems subsequent to *New Poems*; and above all (3) a holograph sheet discovered by Professor Bradford in 'the file envelope containing the surviving MSS of *Responsibilities*' (1914), a 'manuscript table of contents' in Yeats's hand listing 'by number and title' precisely the poems included in, in precisely the order they are given in, the Cuala Press edition[9] (which even perpetuates a slip in the list: 'The Circus Animal's Desertion'):

> Under Ben Bulben
> Three Songs to One Burden (*sic*)
> The Black Tower
> Cuchulain Comforted
> Three Marching Songs
> In Tara's Halls
> The Statues
> News for the Delphic Oracle
> The Long Legged Fly (*sic*)

A Bronze Head
A Stick of Incense
Hound Voice
John Kinsella's Lament etc. (*sic*)
High Talk
The Apparitions
A Nativity
Man and Echo (*sic*)
The Circus Animal's Desertion (*sic*)
Politics

The differences from the corresponding part of what is called *Last Poems* in the standard editions may seem slight : (1) Yeats had excluded the *On the Boiler* poems; (2) he had placed 'Under Ben Bulben' before 'Three Songs to the One Burden,' which in those editions follows directly the last poem in the Cuala Press *New Poems*, 'Are You Content'; (3) he had placed 'The Black Tower' and 'Cuchulain Comforted' before 'Three Marching Songs,' and the three poems that there precede it after it, so that 'Three Marching Songs' stands fifth in both versions; (4) he had placed 'Hound Voice' before, not after 'John Kinsella's Lament for Mrs. Mary Moore'; and (5) he had placed 'The Man and the Echo' before 'The Circus Animals' Desertion' and 'Politics.' Even so, certain consequences of Yeats's having, for example, placed at the beginning, in reverse order, the standard editions' last three poems, and of his also having kept the death poem just before them in those editions ('The Man and the Echo') away from the end of his volume, must be readily apparent. 'Under Ben Bulben' itself, which took him many drafts and more than a month to write, and on which he made changes the night before his final coma, links up effectively to 'Are You Content' of *New Poems*, and epitomizes the subjects, motifs and themes of the volume of poems that it heads to an extent unusual even for him.

Although there seems to be no evidence that the full title of the Cuala Press volume has Yeats's authority, the printing of *The Death of Cuchulain* and *Purgatory* with the poems was by his explicit instructions.[10] This does not compromise the discrete integrity of the group of lyric poems. He was following a practice of combining dramatic 'poems' with apposite literary ones that goes back to the beginning of his career, with *The Wanderings of Oisin and Other Poems* (1889) and *The Countess Kathleen and Various Legends and Lyrics* (1892). The first book published by the Dun Emer Press, the antecedent to the Cuala Press, *In the Seven Woods* (1903), is similar to *Last Poems* in being a coherent group of lyric poems to which *On Baile's Strand* is appended. During his last years *A Full Moon in March* (1935) continued the practice, and poems were published with *The King of the Great Clock Tower* and *The Herne's Egg*. Furthermore, the two plays in *Last Poems and Two Plays* are thoroughly congruent, elucidating sections V and II of 'Under Ben Bulben' respectively.

Beyond reasonable doubt, the generally reliable 'Definitive Edition, With the Author's final Revisions' of *The Collected Poems of W. B. Yeats* ought to have a Table of Contents which lists, following a correct *New Poems* section, 'From ON THE BOILER (1938-9) —' and then 'From LAST POEMS (1939) —,' or else 'From LAST POEMS AND TWO PLAYS (1939) —.' It remains to show how much more than bibliographical authenticity is lost by the persistent critical disregard of this fact.

IV

That coherence in a volume of poetry is satisfying but little else, has been said; and Yeats's achievement in *Last Poems* goes well beyond it. However, the coherence itself is not just a matter of the aptness of a group of poems. Professor Bradford writes: ' "Are You Content?" which echoes the *"siete sodisfatto"* spoken by Shelley's ghost . . . prepares the way for *Last Poems*. . . . Yeats speaks not only "Under Ben Bulben" from the tomb, he speaks all his *Last Poems* from the tomb' (*Yeats's 'Last Poems' Again*, 261). Yeats made the poem with the insistent question which he put at the end of *New Poems*, and which he wrote in his seventy-third year, a virtual promise of more to come. Calling on his ancestors 'To judge what I have done' in his art, he explains: 'Eyes spiritualised by death can judge, / I cannot, but I am not content.' The second stanza catalogues those ancestors and mentions the ancestral graveyard at 'Drumcliff' with

22

LAST POEMS AND TWO PLAYS
BY WILLIAM BUTLER YEATS.

THE CUALA PRESS
DUBLIN IRELAND
MCMXXXIX

Title page of *Last Poems and Two Plays*, The Cuala Press, 1939.

the 'old stone cross' placed there by his Yeats great-grandfather, all key details of his subsequent announcement in 'Under Ben Bulben' that he has joined his ancestors in death.[11] And the last stanza extends the nature of his discontent. In it he says that 'I who have always hated work,' now 'Infirm and aged,' has earned the right to end his life at ease: 'But I am not content.' His discontent is no longer just disquiet about the quality of his art, but a sense as well that it is not complete, he must work on.

In *Last Poems* he declares that his own eyes have become 'spiritualised' by at least impending death and turns and addresses his heirs. The title he gave it, which both complements and contrasts with the neutral *'New Poems,'* announces that the volume of that name comprises the final work of the poet. And so its very coherence makes it the consummation the lack of which he had declared in a poem placed so as to constitute an announcement.

All the poems in the volume were completed during the last year of his life with the exception of 'A Nativity' and possibly 'Three Songs to the One Burden.'[12] A number of critics have demonstrated its interrelations with the later (1937) version of *A Vision*, with his letters of his last year or so (chiefly those to Dorothy Wellesley), and especially with *On the Boiler*. And its principal themes are the preoccupations common to those other documents of the end of his life.

The theme that appears first in *Last Poems* — as the initial article of the 'Under Ben Bulben' 'testament' — is the most pervasive and crucial one. It is the ostensible career of the soul eternally winding and unwinding its mortal wrappings in successive lives and deaths, Yeats's refinement of the vitalist doctrine he evolved decades before with Æ and James Cousins, comrades of the Golden Dawn, and shared not only with Madame Blavatsky but also with golden-thighed Pythagoras and the Druids. Caesar called transmigration of souls the chief Celtic belief, and in Ireland it has had even devout Christians among its adherents.

Although there are hints as early as 'Fergus and the Druid' (1892), the first full expression in his poems of this doctrine is in the volume begun just before the last decade of his life and published (after a partial limited printing under its short title in 1929) as *The Winding Stair and Other Poems* (1933); and the doctrine creates the central

24

antithesis between that volume and its complement, *The Tower* (1928).[13] *The Tower* begins with 'Sailing to Byzantium' declaring that life and the state after life are a simple sequence, the first in and then the other 'out of nature,' the first finite and the other eternal, in the Platonic-Christian tradition. This orthodox doctrine manifestly contradicts Yeats's cyclical paradigm for all existence as much as it does the specific doctrine of reincarnation, and he had committed himself to both three years earlier, in the first version of *A Vision* (1925). Although *A Vision* allows for eventual 'deliverance from birth and death' it is made a distant prospect, not the immediate transcendence expected by the 'aged man' in 'Sailing to Byzantium.' Thus, *The Winding Stair* confronts that innocently monistic poem with an experiential counterpart in 'Byzantium,' in which life and afterlife are portrayed as perpetually successive and contrary states of incarnation and disincarnation.

The second and title poem of *The Tower* elaborates the themes of impending death and subsequent immortality as soul. But the winding staircase in a tower can be descended as well as climbed, and climbed and descended repeatedly. Following the dedicatory 'In Memory of Eva Gore Booth and Con Markiewicz' with its ironically elegiac title, the first two poems in *The Winding Stair* are the short, appropriately named 'Death,' and 'A Dialogue of Self and Soul.' In 'Death' Yeats says definitively about 'a man,' anticipating the first line of the relevant section of 'Under Ben Bulben': 'Many times he died, / Many times rose again.' And in 'A Dialogue of Self and Soul' he elucidates the relationship between *The Winding Stair* and *The Tower*. The 'dialogue' begins with 'My Soul' 'summon[ing] to the winding ancient stair' and the 'breathless starlit air' beyond the top of the tower. But 'My Self' resists the summons, opposing to the central symbol of *The Tower* a minor element in that preceding volume: Sato's sword and the flowered dress fragment 'wound' around its scabbard. 'My Soul' again recommends 'ancestral night that can, / . . . / Deliver from the crime of death and birth.' 'My Self' speaks again of the symbol of the male principle of enduring life enveloped, in a gyre pattern, by the 'flowers' of the female principle, and responds:

> all these I set
> For emblems of the day against the tower
> Emblematical of the night,
> And claim as by a soldier's right
> A charter to commit the crime once more.

Thereupon 'My Soul' expresses the loss of his former certainty, and the dialogue as such ends. The integrated 'self,' spirit and body perpetually wedded, speaks the whole second part of the poem, in which he declares: 'I am content to live it all again / And yet again.'

There is considerable evidence that *The Winding Stair* signifies an unequivocal commitment by the aging Yeats to belief in reincarnation. Although the edition was only a private one of six hundred copies, and although his treatment of death and reincarnation is less prominent there than in the later version, he nevertheless had proclaimed that belief already in *A Vision*. His dedication to *The Winding Stair* takes the trouble of implying that none of the poems concerned with reincarnation was 'written before the publication of *The Tower*'; and the evidence indicates that those poems were begun only after the poems of *The Tower* were finished. In a letter to Mrs. Shakespear he wrote of an early draft of 'A Dialogue of Self and Soul' as 'a choice of rebirth rather than deliverance from birth' (*Letters*, p. 729). Most persuasive perhaps: the final poem of *The Tower*, 'All Souls' Night,' is also the Epilogue to *A Vision*; and in it he announces: 'I have a marvellous thing to say, / A certain marvellous thing / *None but the living* mock' (italics mine), and later, clarifying that: 'I have mummy truths to tell / Whereat the living mock.'

The evidence is not sufficient. Yeats chose to publish *The Tower*, affirming a contrary view of the relationship of the soul and its mortal life, three years after publication of *A Vision*; and he carefully made *The Winding Stair* complementary to it, creating the most elaborate 'tension of opposites' in his poetry. However, the evidence does reveal a strong prior inclination in his thought toward the eventual 'conviction' that 'Many times man lives and dies,' which he was to proclaim, beginning with those words echoing 'Death,' in the initial article of the 'testament' at the head of *Last Poems*. And so it confirms his sincerity respecting that most pervasive and crucial theme of the volume.

As Yeats orders the themes of *Last Poems* blatantly in 'Under Ben Bulben' they are : man's destiny of death and reincarnation (II); the need for sexuality and violence in life ('lust' and 'rage' were two favourite words of his old age, to denote two favoured and linked states of being), (III); the need for sexuality and thought in art (IV); the need to cherish the Irish heritage, which honours and preserves this 'European' way of life and art until its approaching new dispensation (V); and the proper conduct of dying (VI). To these themes must be added a concern — calling it a theme would misrepresent his relationship to it and its powerful changing role in the volume — the death that a few years before in 'After Long Silence' he calmly could belittle as 'unfriendly night.'

The volume perpetuates his familiar iconography : traditional symbols and metaphors like representing the spirit as a bird, which goes back at least as far as the ancient Egyptian *ikhu*; personal ones like the antithetical moon, the wind of imminent historical change, dusk and dawn, walking and climbing; persons like the tinker, the tramp and heroic individuals out of history or myth. But it employs this iconography in its own way. The statues of Phidias and the Sistine Chapel ceiling of Michelangelo, the only great art explicitly cited in the crucial stanza of 'Under Ben Bulben' IV, are prominent in 'The Statues' and 'Long-Legged Fly' respectively. The images of Cuchulain and the social alien are renewed in a number of the more public poems : Cuchulain is linked to the blood sacrifice of the Post Office; and there is a motif of the lusty violent old Irishman being hanged. In addition, the special concerns of *Last Poems* generated patterns of unique imagery. For example, complementing the violent deaths of the politically faithful, lying down and being 'under' are spoken of recurrently in the more personal poems.

Appropriately for a volume the poet saw as consummating his career and making him 'content,' it contains almost every prosodic form he had previously used — including the strong-stress line, the loose and the strict tetrameter, blank verse, the closed couplet, the rhymed irregular line, the six-line stanza, ballad metre, the sonnet, *ottava rima*, the quatrain — and two traditional forms not to be found in his earlier poetry, *terza rima* and rime royal.[14] That in employing those two forms he was not merely avoiding in a per-

27

functory way the absence of distinguished traditional metres from his poetry is shown by the uses to which he put them. The stanza of Dante's poem about the time after death he used in his own poem on the same subject, 'Cuchulain Comforted.' The stanza of *Troilus and Criseyde* and *The Rape of Lucrece* he used for the poems about Maud Gonne and the other 'women I have loved,' 'A Bronze Head' and 'Hound Voice.'

Perhaps most among the elements creating coherence in the volume, its compendium of prosodic forms exemplifies the maker at his last, calculating and shaping. This is so even in his orthodox modernist dependence, for both the anthology of his own characteristic forms and the two traditional ones new to him to achieve their effect, on allusion. And awareness of what he has wrought in its prosody ought to contribute to one's total experience of *Last Poems*.

The principal instrument of coherence, and the principal source of pleasure in the apprehension of it as well, must be the structure of relationships within the volume. Any sketch of the sequence of poems will crudely simplify that structure for a number of reasons. To begin with it is reciprocal, and spatial or simultaneous, as much as it is sequential. Also, much that it achieves is too rich for brief exposition. But above all, no simple account of the poems themselves, some of which have been the subject of extensive critical discussion and of controversy, can pretend to do more than vulgarize them. Such an account sins by both commission and omission. Much of what must be mentioned is either self-evident or already pointed out by others. On the other hand: nothing can be said about complicated matters like the background of 'The Black Tower,' which has been linked with Rosicrucian symbolism, the Arthurian tradition, Shelley, Browning, Irish history and legend, and Yeats's own Thoor Ballylee; and Yeats's enviable ability, exemplified in that poem and others, of combining the personal with the public and grounding both in cosmological vision, must be ignored. Nevertheless, presented in full awareness that what is said about the poems in it is not very likely to exhaust the things that might be said, the following sketch may be useful as articulating by the dominant colour of each the strands of the pattern Yeats has woven.

28

'UNDER BEN BULBEN'

As 'Are You Content' solicited the wisdom of the poet's personal ancestors for himself, so the poem Yeats caused to follow it in the canon, and to complement it, declares the wisdom of their common spiritual ancestors to his spiritual descendants. The first part of the 'testament,' declaring man's destiny of reincarnation, and the fifth part, declaring the readiness of the spirit that had been the buried Yeats to be thrust 'Back in the human mind again,' are related. So are the second, declaring the necessity for violence in human affairs, and the fourth, declaring the value of the Irish heritage as the model of human affairs. The use of references to Phidias and Michelangelo in the central section, devoted to art, has been mentioned. Similar precise verbal linkings to subsequent poems are prepared in the other sections. And because the relationship between 'Under Ben Bulben' and what follows is more direct than is the case with most of his introductory poems, the associations made between sections of it and the appropriate poems are more explicit.

'THREE SONGS TO THE ONE BURDEN,' 'THE BLACK TOWER,'
'CUCHULAIN COMFORTED,' 'THREE MARCHING SONGS,'
'IN TARA'S HALLS'

Thus it is that the next poem has for refrain in all three songs, *'From mountain to mountain ride the fierce horsemen.'* Yeats's familiar equestrian image for the traditional and aristocratic has been enriched in the beginning and in the last line of 'Under Ben Bulben.' Those Irish immortals who ride 'Where Ben Bulben sets the scene,' and embody man's 'eternity' of 'race,' create an appropriate refrain for a set of songs by three very old men about Ireland's noble heritage of virility, community and patriotism unto death.

'The Black Tower' reasserts these values in a dramatic situation. Although 'we' remain 'on guard oath-bound' in the face of apparent defeat and destruction, the line in the refrain: *'But wind comes up from the shore'* (to revitalize 'old bones') intimates hope for a cyclical resurgence. And this modification of pessimism is reinforced by Yeats's placement of the poem before 'Cuchulain Comforted,' in which the arch-hero has begun the process of preparing for an eventual rebirth in the round of human lives and of deaths between them, and before the next poem, 'Three Marching Songs.'

'Three Marching Songs' is subtly changed from the simple hortatory earlier version Yeats had written for O'Duffy's native Fascists, that poet-intellectual's fantasy which Hitler's brown-shirts fulfilled parodically in the interim. Now in each of its songs there is 'creative conflict' between the revised alternative stanzas and a new refrain. For example, *'Drown all the dogs . . .'* has become *'Be still, be still, what can be said?'* Usually a tensional polarity in Yeats's poetry, in this doctrinal last volume the conflict of opposites is more often dialectical, moving forward to a resolution; and 'Three Marching Songs' declares again the values of 'Three Songs to the One Burden.' It moves from a debate between the generations about betraying the heritage in the first song, to the advocacy of violence in 'a good strong cause' in the third, after the last stanza of the second indicates that the time for violence is imminent. The stanza does so by identifying Yeats's wind of historical change with the 'fierce horsemen' of the mountains in the other 'three songs' poem, calling it 'a marching wind,' to answer the question in the refrain : *'What marches down the mountain pass?'*

'In Tara's Halls' is the last of the five consecutive public poems about life and death in Ireland. An important person at the court of the High Kings of ancient Ireland, not necessarily the king, is praised for dying proudly and ceremoniously ('Cast a cold eye / On life, on death').

'THE STATUES,' 'NEWS FOR THE DELPHIC ORACLE,'
'LONG-LEGGED FLY'

The next three poems in the volume are after 'Under Ben Bulben' the most philosophical, in the sense of making explicit general assertions, and are closely related in other ways. The 'news' immediately referred to in the flippant title of the middle one — that Plotinus has successfully completed his swim of 'The Delphic Oracle Upon Plotinus' and joined the 'Golden Race' in the place beyond the sea — becomes trivial beside the dramatic surprise of the momentous 'news' the poem gradually discloses : contrary to the oracle's belief, Plotinus's expectation, and the doctrine declared in 'Sailing to Byzantium,' death is no passage from the temporal 'sensual music' of mortal life to an eternity as 'unageing intellect.' And not only the simple monistic sequence but the very conception of the two states is in error. The oracle's 'Golden' heroes of intellect turn out to be 'golden codgers' and 'Innocents' carried to that ultramarine 'country' by the dolphins of the vision depicted in 'Byzantium'; the 'choir of Love' are nymphs and satyrs; Pan is the reigning deity; and sexual generation 'in the foam' is the homage his sensual music exacts and the actual agent of human immortality. Thus, with appropriate suggestiveness, 'the brute dolphins plunge / Until . . . / . . . / They pitch their burdens off.'

After imparting its general news about the place, the poem reports of one specific pair of lovers. Thetis, the nymph who became the mother of Achilles, has stripped Peleus, the mortal who became his father; she is subject to the sovereignty of Pan; finally, on his signal her sister Nereides couple with satyrs. The reflexive implication that she also does so or will do so with Peleus, like the innuendo of a gossip-journalist's 'news,' achieves more emphasis than would direct statement. This depiction of the time immediately before the life of the Achaeans' arch-hero is a precise complement in the volume for the poem about the time immediately after the death of his Irish counterpart.

Yeats speaks in *A Vision* of six states of the spirit between lives. 'Cuchulain Comforted' portrays an early state, and the more conventional part of his doctrine, which is that in the early states of any death, a man's spirit moves away from his (last) mortality towards 'My soul's first shape, a soft feathery shape,' as Cuchulain expresses it in the play about his death appended to the poems. 'News for the Delphic Oracle' portrays the more special part of that doctrine (although it seems to have affinities with Blake's *Book of Thel* and with Wordsworth), the circumstances of the last state of a man's transitory death, in which his spirit approaches his next mortality.

Like the poems at either side of it, which elucidate 'Under Ben Bulben' on art, 'News for the Delphic Oracle' elucidates 'Under Ben Bulben' on the 'brief parting' of death. And it relates to them because of the stress, common to all three, on the role of our human sexuality in our affairs, civilization and individual destinies. Elaborating Yeats's doctrine of reincarnation proclaimed in 'Under Ben Bulben,' 'News for the Delphic Oracle' declares that one's dead spirit will receive a new 'Husk' and 'Passionate Body' (his terms in *A Vision*) and come into life again through the power of, quite fittingly, sexual pro-creation. The relative power of blood and the dance is reversed from that at the beginning of the period of death, at which time, as 'Byzantium' puts it, 'The marbles of the dancing floor / Break bitter furies of complexity.' Furthermore, 'News for the Delphic Oracle' combines with the two poems that frame it to declare that the sexuality they all stress is the vehicle for the reciprocal relationship between art and life.

In the opening stanza of 'The Statues,' 'passion' is said to bring the necessary (ideally austere) 'character' to art, and reciprocally the art created, whether the fantasies of boys and girls in bed or the 'plummet-measured face' they are moved to kiss, is said to engender sexuality. Yeats's casual allusion in the poem following these three, 'A Bronze Head,' to a head of Maud Gonne in Dublin's Municipal Gallery of Modern Art, is one more exclusivist Irish trait in the volume. But at least a 'bronze Head' is mentioned. 'News for the Delphic Oracle' says nothing about pictures; yet a male figure on the shore being embraced by an assertive female, in a setting that has both a pipes player and pairs of nymphs and satyrs in shallow water, can be seen in a painting by Poussin in the National Gallery of Ireland which is part of the Lane bequest, and which in Yeats's later years was entitled 'The Marriage of Peleus and Thetis.' [15] By adapting his sexual account of the parents of Achilles to that Renaissance picture, Yeats achieves in the poem a second larger purpose for his volume: the assertion, immediately following 'The Statues,' of the vital role the sexual imagination had in Poussin's creation.

Furthermore, the doctrine which in 'The Statues' (and in the wider reference of 'the sexual instinct of Europe') is presented as the corollary to this one, the radical Aestheticism expressed in the command to artists in 'Under Ben Bulben' that they cause men to 'fill the cradles right,' then hinted again facetiously a few lines below with the 'globe-trotting Madam' whose 'bowels' are put 'in heat' by the 'half-awakened Adam' of the Sistine Chapel ceiling, is elucidated in 'Long-Legged Fly.' It declares that Michelangelo must work speci-fically so 'That girls at puberty may find / The first Adam in their thought.' Art is created out of sexuality and mind; art generates and guides sexuality, and so perpetuates life and enables, in the words of *The King's Threshold*, 'triumphant children.' In a sense, the three poems constitute the centre of gravity of the volume.

'A BRONZE HEAD,' 'A STICK OF INCENSE,' 'HOUND VOICE,'
'JOHN KINSELLA'S LAMENT FOR MRS. MARY MOORE'

The next four poems are a group about the love of women and about loss. The two in rime-royal, quasi-elegies in which the lives of the women celebrated are spoken of as though essentially ended, are the first poems in the volume with any explicit personal reference. Even 'Under Ben Bulben,' which presented the poet's testament, mentioned his burial and published his epitaph, referred impersonally to 'Yeats' and 'his command.' The two poems about Marys that alternate with them contrast with them as well; for those assert the primacy of sexual love and also, appropriately, are simple in manner, although the ballad is a more moving elegy than either of the two elevated and spiritualized personal tributes.

The four poems have various of the familiar elements of coherence in the volume, but almost perfunctorily. 'A Bronze Head' deals with age, death and 'Ancestral pearls pitched into [the modern] sty.' 'A Stick of Incense,' whose title is an ironic pun that suggests a religious tribute to make a sexual one, retells a portion of the myth of the Nativity in realistic terms, like the poet's earlier 'The Mother of God.' It relates to 'A Nativity,' but more meaningful for the volume is its central blasphemy asserting the importance of sexuality in human experience. The spirit of 'the Hound of Culann' is transformed in 'Cuchulain Comforted' and 'summoned' to the Post Office by Padraic Pearse in 'The Statues'; these explicit representations of the hero are repeated respectively in the passage already quoted from *The Death of Cuchulain* and the 'harlot's song' at the end of the play. However, the volume augments these representations with oblique allusions: in the last of 'Three Songs to the One Burden,' in 'News for the Delphic Oracle,' and in the lyric about Yeats and his women, loyal to their Irish heritage and 'companioned by a hound,' 'Hound Voice.' Finally, 'John Kinsella's Lament for Mrs. Mary Moore' begins with a repetition of a familiar motif, an old man speaking of violent death.

33

It is no accident that the group of poems in which the first explicit personal references in the volume occur also have relatively weak links to the preceding poems, which cohere so closely through the doctrinal themes introduced in 'Under Ben Bulben.' For the personal element, the concern that is no such theme, mentioned earlier, is a new and alternative principle of coherence in *Last Poems*. It enters the volume at midpoint, with the tenth poem, 'A Bronze Head.' And it engages the doctrinal element in 'creative conflict' with increasing power to the end.

'HIGH TALK,' 'THE APPARITIONS,' 'A NATIVITY,' 'THE MAN AND THE ECHO'

Following five public poems, three philosophical ones, and four about the love of women and loss the first and third of which concern women important in Yeats's own life, the volume presents a group of four lyrics about artistic creation and the approaching death of their creator. Of the final six lyrics, the only one in which the speaker does not explicitly identify himself as the poet making an intimate declaration is 'A Nativity.' It is also one of the very few poems in the volume that neither gain much from nor contribute much to *Last Poems* as an entity. Its two couplets about the real Nativity framing four about the power of artists seem to assert that art established and preserves the central myth of our civilization. It does correspond to 'High Talk' and contrast with the poems on either side of itself to form a group with an alternating pattern similar to that of the preceding group of four alternately personal and impersonal, elegiac and sexual, poems. The two poems expressing confidence in the power of art to transcend mortality alternate with those expressing a man's confrontation with the once merely unfriendly 'increasing Night / That opens her mystery and fright.'

This alternation represents in little the relationship that evolves in *Last Poems* between the poetic declarations of the *seanchan* which dominate the first half of the volume and the voice of the dying man which is the chief agency of coherence in the second half. The description may suggest an almost neat division, but what Yeats achieves in fact is an unfolding confrontation; and the symbolic action it creates is the object of this study.

34

The two concluding poems make the poet's final statements as artist and as man respectively.

The above sketch of the relationships of the poems gives a general impression of neatness, a work of calculation which is at worst life- less and at best only pleasing. Furthermore, there no doubt are other possible conceptions of subordinate groupings in the volume. The only alternative I can conceive would be even neater, with four groups of four poems between 'Under Ben Bulben' and the final pair. (It joins 'In Tara's Halls' to 'The Statues,' 'News for the Delphic Oracle' and 'Long-Legged Fly' as poems about the relationship of art and life.) Finally, the groups are not discrete and schematic. The volume modulates from one to another, so that in addition to its other inadequacies any sketch is partly a misrepresentation. For example, in 'Long-Legged Fly' Helen is called 'three parts a child,' and an incongruous Irish metaphor describes her dancing as a 'tinker's shuffle,' to connect that poem with the next, 'A Bronze Head,' which I have said begins another group, and in which Yeats speaks of having called his Irish Helen 'My child, my child!' With its contrast between the assured public poet pronouncing a judgement on Helen of Troy and the man who once exclaimed so about his beloved, this example also shows, at the point at which it begins — for 'A Bronze Head' is the first explicitly personal poem in the volume — the confrontation that *Last Poems* ultimately is about.

V

Of general importance because Yeats wrote them, but more important here because they contribute to its creation, is the recip- rocal effect the whole of *Last Poems* has on some of the individual poems it comprises. Aside from making more acceptable the patches of poor verse in (most notably) 'Under Ben Bulben,' 'The Statues' and 'The Apparitions,' because the lapses are not only prominent parts of small works but also tiny parts of a large one, that effect is chiefly of two kinds. As the unity of *Last Poems* reveals itself, it reveals also the clarity of the apparently obscure and the richness of the appar- ently slight.

'Cuchulain Comforted' has seemed just such an obscure poem. Various determinations of Cuchulain's ghostly status have been made from Yeats's discussion of the human spirit between its lives in *A Vision* ('Book III: The Soul in Judgment'); but these are not very enlightening. The only essential element of Yeats's cosmology is that humans move through death toward reincarnation as they move through life toward death. And that element is already present in *Last Poems* itself, while the real difficulty with the poem is precisely what Cuchulain's comfort is.

The great Irish hero seems to be paying a hard (and curious) price for it if his comfort is merely that his spirit moves toward its next state once he has accepted the company of the 'cowards' in death. Change to a new and equally transitory state in an unalterable process is not very comforting. It is not even relief for Cuchulain, since he is not suffering. And if his comfort is that the process exists, and his death *is* only transitory, why is the company of cowards in the poem?

However, 'Cuchulain Comforted' has a certain place in a larger entity. All three preceding poems have denounced the unfaithful 'louts' who dominate Ireland, and asserted optimism about her ultimate triumph through a resurgence of her ancient values. Now the hero is confronted by just such flawed Irishmen. Their leader's statement that 'Your life will grow much sweeter' if he will 'make a shroud' cannot mean simply that he will begin the comforting process of moving through death after completing his shroud. Aside from the reasons given, this is so both because he is transformed after he only 'began to sew,' and because when the leader speaks the shrouds of the degraded company are already completed, yet they remain untransformed. It is as though they have been waiting for him. And when he consents to join them the mere fact enables them to change 'in common' with him, as though his *virtu* effects their transformation as well. 'Cuchulain Comforted' is among the group of public poems, and the arch-hero's comfort is ultimately political. He is portrayed more than once in *Last Poems* as inspiring Irish heroism. What comforts him is that he has not died to Ireland. Because he joined them in death the attachment of his new companions to their past degradation has ended and their movement toward new life begun. When they are 'thrust' back on earth it will be as Irishmen purified of former cowardice, able to stand in the Post Office and the black tower.

A poem so slight in isolation as to command no special attention is 'In Tara's Halls,' the 'praise' of an old man who, sensing its approach, spends a year preparing for and then performs the ceremony of his death:

> Summoned the generations of his house,
> Lay in the coffin, stopped his breath and died.

It has seemed to critics merely the retelling of an ancient legend of uncertain origin. However, as the last of a group of poems about public matters by Ireland's *seanchan* and/or the first of a group about the relationship of life and art, in a unified work called *Last Poems* that occupied the final year of his life, it explains both the mystery of its supposed source and the alteration Yeats made in manuscript from 'a certain king' to 'a man.' [16] The man the poet praises for announcing his end in 'the Sacred House' and then preparing for and consummating that death with ceremony is himself; these are the things he did in creating *Last Poems*. 'In Tara's Halls' characterizes the volume and celebrates it. And its seriousness and richness are shorn away if the poem is isolated from the larger entity that is both its setting and its occasion.

The old man praised in 'In Tara's Halls' concerns himself not at all with possibly uncompleted affairs of the life he is about to leave, but only with the death before him. So throughout *Last Poems* Yeats only faces ahead, toward death and what lies beyond. The introductory section of 'Under Ben Bulben' catalogues the Witch of Atlas and the sages of ancient Egypt, all gnostics of the time after life, and then the 'pale' Irish in that existence as spirit. The sages 'set the cocks' of reawakening 'acrow'; the 'company' of Irish spirits 'ride the wintry dawn' of imminent new life. In the 'testament' that follows, art enjoys the honour of the central position; but the opening and closing lines are the couplet:

> Many times man lives and dies
> Between his two eternities,

and the poet's actual epitaph :

> *Cast a cold eye*
> *On life, on death.*
> *Horseman, pass by !*

Aside from any functional reason, the pointed impersonality of his references to himself just before the epitaph dramatically expresses the firm conviction from which all the other beliefs declared in the poem are explicitly said by its first dozen lines to derive, and in which they are implicitly said by the epitaph to culminate. Since 'Yeats' both in the poem and in fact has died, then what was the poet is now spirit between lives, must have left that former identity. 'I' commands his heirs to 'swear' from beyond the grave at the beginning of the poem, but the 'command' the dead poet once gave for the cutting of the gravestone, mentioned at the end, is 'his'.

As the special place allotted it in 'Under Ben Bulben' might suggest, the relationship of life and death is the pervasive subject of *Last Poems*; and in fact every single poem in the volume explicitly deals with either the ending or the beginning of life. That is another reason why at least two of the three poems in *On the Boiler* were not included, and the reason why Yeats reprinted *Purgatory* from the pamphlet.

What Yeats does with the pervasive subject of his volume is the moving achievement that compelled the writing of this study. It has been said that through the first half of *Last Poems* he avoided personal references, and that the essential nature of the volume is realized only when the personal element appears. Gradually a relationship evolves between the new expressed feelings of the man, and the assured public declarations of the Poet and Thinker which they interrupt. The opposing aspects of his self are Yeats's familiar antitheses. It is only that one of them attempted to assert a univocal stance in the volume; and the mortal dancer will not be denied. An index of what happens is the contrast between the Poet's calm placement of 'I' beyond the grave in 'Under Ben Bulben' and those nakedly personal poems of the still-dying old man that begin with 'A Bronze Head.' With 'High Talk' they become uninterrupted except by 'A Nativity' through to the end. And toward the end they fasten unceremoniously on the imminent death which the man of Tara, whom the assured Poet has praised as his surrogate, confronted so differently. Within the very volume 'Under Ben Bulben' introduces, Yeats himself fails to obey his final injunction to 'the generations of his house' made in that poem, that they 'Cast a cold eye / On life, on death,' and belies the epitaph he declares is cut in stone over his grave.

This change during the course of *Last Poems* could be mere inconsistency. But the demonstrable integrity of the volume alone indicates that Yeats did create a relationship. One of the contraries having been suppressed and increasingly obtruding itself, the relationship can only be one of conflict. In fact it is made high drama.

The complication unfolds quietly in the first poem of the final group of four, the sonnet of couplets, 'High Talk.' The octave begins 'Processions that lack high stilts have nothing that catches the eye' and ends 'I take to chisel and plane.' The sestet portrays the resulting 'procession'. In it, both the great Irish Poet who is himself the speaker ('Malachi Stilt-Jack am I') and his art ('no modern stalks upon higher') are designated 'metaphor'; promptly, the sonnet becomes a procession of metaphors. The 'light' through which he 'stalks' on his stilts, called a 'terrible novelty' because life is transitory when it occurs, is contrasted to the approach being made to a new dawn by the barnacle goose and seahorses in their 'night'.

Yeats's account in the sestet of his procession through life is of a master artist's career. It is undeniably high talk, not just describes but metaphorically is the procession on stilts whose creation he announced at the end of the octave. However, it is more resigned than triumphant. The octave has declared that the stilts are made and used for others. He is obliged to 'stalk' unnaturally through life as he does for the sake of 'show,' because others 'demand'; and he proceeds toward the night, not the new dawn. Thus, the title signifies not only the poetic accomplishment of the metaphorical sestet but also its elevation above normal human reality. Beyond the night he must reach he will find eventually a new dawn, the dying Poet declares while on his stilts, but his familiar calm assurance about the future is subtly compromised by the characterization of all such 'stilts' as 'metaphor.' And that characterization is reinforced by a blatant denigration of the 'creative intellect' planted in the octave's apparent praise of it. The reference there to 'Daddy-long-legs upon his timber toes' is to a long-legged fly, but one whose legs are not now characterized as an integral part of him.

The next lyric, 'The Apparitions,' turns from the first of the two alternating themes in the group, the power of art, to the second, the confrontation with approaching death. The fifteenth poem in the volume, its strength is in its terrible refrain :

> Fifteen apparitions have I seen;
> The worst a coat upon a coat-hanger.

And that this explicit assertion of the distress about his human mortality which began subtly to attack the confident artist and sage in 'High Talk' has indeed brought him low, is indicated by the movement from fifteen-foot stilts to fifteen apparitions.

'The Man and the Echo' follows the impersonal and unequivocal assertion of the power of art in 'A Nativity,' and is the second poem about Yeats the man's confrontation with death. With its guilty brooding over *Cathleen Ni Houlihan*, Margot Ruddock and Lady Gregory's estate, it is explicitly personal. In 'Vacillation' he had said that when life ends: 'The body calls it death, / The heart remorse. / But if these be right / What is joy?' As sexuality anticipates the return to life in 'News for the Delphic Oracle,' so in 'The Man and the Echo' does 'remorse' anticipate the death in which the spirit must resolve remorse. Like 'Cuchulain Comforted,' the poem deals with 'that which cleans man's dirty slate' and frees one's spirit to move past the first purgatorial state of death. The process of thought he portrays is reflected by the two commands of the 'Rocky Voice'. The first, 'Lie down and die,' follows his complaint in the first stanza that he would prefer death to the futile questionings of his insomniac remorse; and the echo in turn causes him to declare in the second stanza that dying would not end the process, for it must be undergone even in death until it is completed. Only then one 'sinks at last into the night,' fully beyond one's past life. Following the echo's 'Into the night,' he asks if that full spirit state is the 'joy' which 'Vacillation' wondered about. Then suddenly in this third stanza the activity of the 'spiritual intellect,' which began as remorse in preparation for the state after death, and evolved first into an exposition of the process of purgatorial remorse itself, and then into questions about the state for which it prepares, is ended. He has 'lost the theme' because of the death cry of 'a stricken rabbit'; for the first time within a single poem, the brutal fact of his approaching death explicitly overwhelms his convictions and his control.

'The Circus Animals' Desertion' and 'Politics,' the final statements of the Poet and the man, are affected by their large context in much the same way as are 'Cuchulain Comforted' and 'In Tara's Halls' respectively. The final poem is richer than it seems in isolation; the position alone of the final statement of the Poet discredits optimistic readings its apparent obscurities have generated. 'The Circus Animals' Desertion' is impressive, but it is not essentially a reaffirmation of the power of the artist in old age.

The conflict that has developed between the stance of the assured artist and sage which dominates the first part of the volume and the human being's fears of death, increasingly obtrusive and just portrayed as dominant, is confronted directly in 'The Circus Animals' Desertion.' The crucial element of the poem is the expression of precisely that high drama, in the opposed metaphors 'heart' and 'dream.' Yeats's two familiar antithetical aspects he characterizes as his 'heart' and as the 'pure mind' that gave him 'themes' for works of art which, when created, became 'circus animals' to others and to himself 'dreams,' much like the 'images' or 'Presences' of 'Among School Children': alternatives to the human realities of his heart.

The single stanza which is the poem's first section immediately uses the word 'theme,' so prominent at the end of the preceding poem, and there made to characterize the process and the formulations of intellect. The stanza promptly sets up the antithesis with 'my heart,' makes clear that 'theme' here has to do with the artist's 'creative intellect,' and then directly links this poem to 'High Talk.' The 'circus animals' metaphor recalls the 'piebald ponies, led bears, caged lions' accompanying 'Malachi Stilt-Jack'; and placed first in the circus procession are 'Those stilted boys.'

The second section of the poem ostensibly is intended only to 'enumerate old themes,' new inspiration being lacking, with one

41

'theme' allotted to each of its three stanzas. But description becomes analysis and then introspection. Each of the three long early works he describes is said to have ultimately distracted him from what should have been his human feelings:

> Heart-mysteries there, and yet when all is said
> It was the dream itself enchanted me.

The final couplet of the third stanza is a general judgement:

> Players and painted stage took all my love,
> And not those things that they were emblems of.

Again a single stanza, the third section draws the conclusion that has been prepared for. The 'masterful images . . . / Grew in pure mind,' but began in 'the foul rag-and-bone shop of the heart' — those human feelings that 'they were emblems of.' In this final section the association with 'High Talk' invoked earlier comes into play to alter the portrayal he made there of Yeats the poet. Stilts are a means of public performance, and his art was there characterized as principally that. But although, as he says, it may provide a circus 'show,' a ladder is primarily personal, a means of climbing upward. He used his art when young as the means to climb away from his human reality. He escaped with Oisin's 'faery bride' from 'the embittered heart' of frustration, with Countess Cathleen from his unrequited love for his 'dear,' with the great Cuchulain from political disappointment. Now he is suffering once more and such escape has been taken from him. Forever in this life: one does not lie down where ladders start, as the famous next-to-last line declares that he must do, if one expects to be climbing, or anticipates that another ladder will replace the one that is 'gone'; and the final statement of the artist about his art in *Last Poems* nowhere suggests that he expects new 'Themes' in the future. The thought of his death obliterated the 'theme' in 'The Man and the Echo'; in this next poem, 'at last, being but a broken man, / I must be satisfied with my heart.' He 'must' lie down in his present human condition, as its two last lines say: he must confront in his art his heart's true subject, his inescapable suffering over the approach of death, because that imminent death itself has deprived him of the escape ladder of 'themes' or 'masterful images.' What in the early part of the volume had been presented confidently as a gifted individual's own long legs of creative intellect, then as stilts, is now something completely external to the old man, and simply taken away. The poem is an apologia for the nakedly personal nature of those that precede it and the brief final lyric that follows it.

That confrontation which he says he no longer can avoid as subject for his poetry is deftly incorporated into the poem itself. He does not choose to but 'must lie down.' One normally is not obliged to do so as a consequence of lacking a ladder for climbing, or even any future prospect of one. Echoing 'I / Sleepless would lie down and die' of 'The Man and the Echo,' the phrase is as significant here as it becomes by the end of the medieval ballad 'Lord Randal.'

The drama of Yeats's confrontation with his approaching death is augmented further. He is not proud of the use to which he put his creative power when young. And when the ladder of escape from his feelings is most needed he accepts his deprivation no longer with terror but with stoic resignation. The final poem, 'Politics,' embodying a triple reversal, a richness revealed only when it is restored to its proper context, takes that drama to its end.

One reversal is precisely of the stoic resignation. Not terror again but yearning supplants it, in a sudden final appeal that recalls Faustus's final 'Ile burne my bookes.' Using language so simple and direct it is itself a shock after the many rich and complicated poems, he talks apparently calmly about his difference with the epigraph from Thomas Mann, calling politics unimportant when compared with the most elementary sensual love, then suddenly makes his final extravagant exclamation. His wish to be 'young again' is a last expression of the feelings of the dying man who is resisting the injunction of his own epitaph that one 'cast a cold eye': 'But O' he cries, if only he were living this life of William Butler Yeats again.

However, the doctrine of reincarnation is his own; and despite terror, suffering and appeal he nowhere renounces it. The conflict in *Last Poems* has arisen from the initial attempt by his 'pure mind' to deny his 'heart'; and its failure to do so neither discredits nor compromises the 'convictions' of the assured Poet in him, merely defeats the sovereignty over his dying that the artist and sage tried to assert. The second reversal is muted, but there, hovering above the moving final craving for life. Since the heart's appeal of the man Yeats does not invalidate the doctrine of the gnostic so sincerely held that it literally is, as it is said to be by the introductory poem of the volume, the subject of his epitaph, that doctrine affirms that the essential 'I' shall be young 'again' and again.

The third reversal also qualifies the end of the drama of the artist and sage increasingly defeated by the man's mortality. It is a subtle final assertion of artistic power. The artistry of the Poet has linked this apparently simple lyric glorifying sexuality to one of the most complex in the volume, appropriately the most explicitly sexual poem Yeats ever published, 'News for the Delphic Oracle.' For the form of this plain direct statement is a complex twelve-line stanza alternating longer and shorter lines, with the alternate shorter lines rhymed in three pairs—precisely the stanza of 'News for the Delphic Oracle.' As the doctrine persists, so the art endures, and in its own realm at least, triumphs.

Last Poems is the posthumous final volume by Yeats which represents itself as the work of a confident poet and thinker, but in which things begin to happen, caused by human fears and suffering that the initial elevated stance is increasingly unable to suppress. The young Yeats called the aspect of him which made that stance its formal public embodiment his 'mask,' and the term is worth recalling for *Last Poems*. Its attempt to conceal fails, and his heart is exposed, even to the pitiable nakedness of his last exclamation. The drama is precisely of the kind Donne achieves in 'Goodfriday, 1613. Riding Westward,' in the progressive stripping away of the speaker's alternative masks until he discloses the truth about his facing away from Christ. And that poem is an Easter confession.

The recent interest in contemporary 'confessional poetry' has tended really to be concerned with poetry which publishes what is normally kept private, often poetry merely of indiscretion or exhibition. For it is not the content of a revelation that makes it a confession rather than an inadvertence or even a boast, but the revealer's own attitude toward it. A reader cannot assume a writer's reluctance to reveal something because he himself would be reluctant

44

to do so. A person disclosing a small social cruelty he imposed on a stranger may be confessing, while another disclosing a terrible cruelty to a lover may be careless, or boasting, or even merely using sensational material as spectacle. Furthermore, where a literary work is concerned, that attitude of reluctance can be said to exist only by being made manifest in it. In genuine confessional literature the attitude of confession, the writer's resistance to telling because of his reluctance to have the matter known, is present as part of the work. And the dramatic conflict between that attempt to mask the matter and the pressure to reveal it, not the nature of the thing revealed, is the essential source of the effect of such art on all but the prying and the prurient.

The very fact that Yeats was willing to create in his volume an action that is truly confessional is itself the final element in that drama of *Last Poems*. For *Last Poems* is tied to his own dying firmly; and in both revealing what any person would conceal and making art of his revelation he died both honestly and therefore nobly as a man, and triumphantly as a poet. The man of Tara had an easier time of it; Yeats's affairs included powerful fears and yearnings. Yet ultimately he does deserve the praise he gave himself in that poem for dying ceremoniously. He set all in order and died with the transfiguring ceremony of *Last Poems*. Very few artists equalled their highest level of accomplishment at the end of a long life. To do so in a work that confronts one's own dying is movingly courageous. As he says of Dante in 'Ego Dominus Tuus,' he set his chisel to the hardest stone.

NOTES ON THE TEXT

1 *On the Boiler* [2nd ed.], (Dublin : Cuala Press, 1939), (reprinted 1971), p. 37.

2 *The Collected Plays of W. B. Yeats* (New York : Macmillan, 1953), p. 73.

3 Hugh Kenner, in 'The Sacred Book of the Arts,' *Gnomon : Essays in Contemporary Literature* (New York : McDowell, Obolensky, 1958), p. 14. John Unterecker's *A Reader's Guide to William Butler Yeats* (New York : Noonday, 1959) applies this conception to the standard edition of the *Collected Poems*.

4 Curtis Bradford, 'The Order of Yeats's *Last Poems*,' *Modern Language Notes*, 76 (1961), 515-16. It is reprinted at the end of his pamphlet, *Yeats's 'Last Poems' Again*, already cited.

5 Ironically, Professor Bradford's pamphlet is reprinted as 'On Yeats's *Last Poems*' in a 'casebook,' *Yeats : Last Poems* (ed. Jon Stallworthy), (London : Macmillan, 1968), which disregards its 'case' and follows the general practice. However, see also pp. 72-73 of the editor's *Vision and Revision . . .*, already cited.

6 W. K. Wimsatt, 'Horses of Wrath : Recent Critical Lessons,' in *Hateful Contraries : Studies in Literature and Criticism* (Lexington : Univ. of Kentucky Press, 1966), pp. 21, 24, 25-26.

7 The poems are 'Why Should Not Old Men Be Mad?,' 'The Statesman's Holiday,' and 'Crazy Jane on the Mountain.' The appropriateness is such that, for example, the last of them, in which Jane laments because George V did not abdicate two decades before when the Russian imperial family was killed, an embarrassingly silly anachronism in the standard editions, is more acceptable as the coda to a discussion of the English monarchy's unfitness to the Irish character.

8 By 13 July 1938 the poet F. R. Higgins, to whom he had given *On the Boiler* with instructions to send it to the printer, had read and commented on the text, although at that time the Crazy Jane poem was not finished. By 4 September the pamphlet was at the printer's. He dated the 'Preface' 'October, 1938.' On 23 December it was 'not yet out,' and he complained of the 'small Longford printer selected in pure eccentricity by the poet Higgins.' (See *The Letters of W. B. Yeats*, ed. Allan Wade [New York : Macmillan, 1955], pp. 912, 915, 921.)

Although the date the first edition of *On the Boiler* actually was completed is not known, Yeats would seem to have been fully familiar with its contents. Months before his death the printer's copy had been prepared and had passed through his hands. He lived five full weeks after his impatient allusion of December 23rd, so that at least galleys of a fifty-page printing project could have been sent to him in the south of France if he had not already seen them before leaving Ireland. Also, the recent list of Cuala Press reprints, and two 'facsimile notes' within the *On the Boiler* (although it is reprinted from the later standard edition), give 1938 as its date. (The edition was suppressed 'by decision of Mrs. Yeats,' perhaps after her return as a widow to Dublin, because of the poor job done by the 'Longford printer'; see Liam Miller, *The Dun Emer Press, Later the Cuala Press* [Dublin : Dolmen Press, 1973], p. 91. The standard edition was not published until the Autumn of 1939; the advertisement follows the text in both editions.)

9   *Yeats's 'Last Poems' Again*, 283, 260. See also : Stallworthy, p. vii, n. 2 and p. 10; and Patrick J. Keane, 'Introduction,' *William Butler Yeats : A Collection of Criticism* (ed. Keane), (New York : McGraw-Hill, 1973), p. 2, n. 2.

10   *Yeats's 'Last Poems' Again*, 284.

11   In fact, his interment at Drumcliff was delayed eight years.

12   *Yeats's 'Last Poems' Again*, 285-86.

13   For an account of the various relations between the two volumes, see Unterecker, pp. 169-240, especially pp. 169-71 and pp. 200-203.

14   See *Yeats's 'Last Poems' Again*, 276-82 for a descriptive review; the 'new form' referred to on 280 is rime royal.

15   In a 1932 catalogue of the National Gallery the painting has that title, and 'Acis and Galatea' is said to be the title formerly given it; the title is unchanged in a 1951 catalogue; in a 1964 catalogue the former (and apparently authentic) title is restored. T. R. Henn says that the *Colloque Poussin* in 1958 authenticated the original title (*The Lonely Tower : Studies in the Poetry of W. B. Yeats* [London : Methuen, 1965], p. 249).

   Although the erroneous title misled Yeats to identify as Pan the pipes-playing and apparently Cyclopean giant figure in the painting (presumably it is Polyphemus), his own portrayal of the mating of Peleus and Thetis is appropriate : in Ovid, *Metamorphoses*, XI, Thetis rides a dolphin to a cavern by the shore, where Peleus eventually wins her.

16   See A. Norman Jeffares, *A Commentary on the Collected Poems of W. B. Yeats* (Stanford : Stanford Univ. Press, 1968), p. 489.

NEW YEATS PAPERS XI

Yeats at His Last deals with the volume of poems which Yeats composed at the end of his life and which the Cuala Press published under the title *Last Poems and Two Plays* in July 1939, almost six months after the poet's death. Professor Sultan reviews the bibliographical and other evidence authenticating the Cuala Press edition; he relates the prevailing disregard of that evidence in favour of the familiar ostensible *Last Poems* to recent critical biases towards Yeats's poetry; and he indicates the limitations of those biases when measured against both Yeats's achievement in the authentic volume and the poetics he enunciated there. In addition, the relationships among them are shown to illuminate a number of the poems, including such controversial ones as 'Cuchulain Comforted', 'The Statues' and 'The Circus Animals' Desertion'. But the greater work which the dying poet wrought of those nineteen lyrics is Professor Sultan's essential subject.

Stanley Sultan, born in Brooklyn, New York, in 1928, is Professor of English Literature at Clark University. He has edited *The Playboy of the Western World*, incorporating changes Synge made during the Abbey rehearsals, has written on Renaissance drama, Synge, William Faulkner and on contemporary American fiction and poetry. He is the author of *The Argument of Ulysses* and other studies of Joyce.

The drawing on the cover is reproduced from the design by Jack B. Yeats for the cover of *On the Boiler*, 1939.

THE DOLMEN PRESS DUBLIN IRELAND

Distributed in the United States of America and in Canada by Humanities Press Inc., 171 First Avenue, Atlantic Highlands, New Jersey 07716, U.S.A.

ISBN 0 85105 271 1   £1.85 *net*

(Price in the Republic of Ireland, including v.a.t. £1.98.)